Ancient Chinese Architecture

First Edition 2002
Second Printing 2005

Ancient Chinese Architecture

ISBN 7-119-03115-5

© Foreign Languages Press
Published by Foreign Languages Press
24 Baiwanzhuang Road, Beijing 100037, China
Home Page: http://www.flp.com.cn
E-mail Addresses: info@flp.com.cn
                sales@flp.com.cn
Distributed by China International Book Trading Corporation
35 Chegongzhuang Xilu, Beijing 100044, China
P.O.Box 399, Beijing ,China

Printed in the People's Republic of China

Ancient Chinese Architecture

By *Lou Qingxi*

Foreign Languages Press Beijing

Contents

Preface

Lou Qingxi

China is a country with a long history, a rich cultural tradition and an ancient civilization. On this land, our ancestors left us an abundance of splendid, time-honored architectural legacy, which has undergone thousands of years of development to become a distinct part of world architectural history. These features are demonstrated mainly in the following aspects:

1. Wooden Framework

Wooden frameworks for buildings appeared at a very early period of Chinese history. First, rows of wooden pillars are raised from the ground, on which horizontal wooden roof beams and crossbeams are placed. The roof timbers are laid on the beams, so

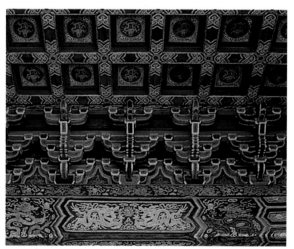

that the weight of the roof is all transmitted to the ground by way of the beams and the upright pillars. The advantages of this form of structure are as follows: First, the wooden framework bears all the weight of the building, which makes the installation of both the outer and inner walls flexible and able to be placed in accordance with practical needs. For example, the outer walls can be substantial, thick and made of bricks or stones in the north, and thin, made of bamboo and wooden planks in the south. Doors and windows can be installed between the erected pillars, or the pillars can be left open. Inside, the house can be divided into spaces with different purposes using wooden partitions and screens. Second, the wooden framework is shock-resistant, because the parts are linked by mortise-and-tenon joints. So, when subjected to a violent shock such as that from an earthquake, a wooden framework is less likely to break or fall down than a brick or stone one. The wooden pagoda at Fogong Temple in Yingxian County, Shanxi Province, is a 67-m-high wooden structure. In its over 900 years of existence it has been jolted by several earthquakes, but it still stands erect and firm. Third, a wooden framework is easy to construct. Wood is a natural material, not like bricks and tiles which are manufactured. Compared with stones which are also natural materials, wood is much easier to obtain, refine and work on. Covering an area of 720,000 sq m and with nearly 1,000 wooden-framework buildings totaling 160,000 sq m, the Forbidden City (the former Imperial Palace) in Beijing, built in its present form in the Ming

Dynasty, took 13 years from the preparation of materials to total completion, in which almost ten years' time was for the preparation of materials, and the time for construction on the spot was no more than three to four years.

Of course, wooden structures also have their disadvantages. Their durability is not as good as structures of brick or stone. Wood is vulnerable to fire and humidity, and attacks by insects. Thus, wooden structures tend to last a shorter time than brick or stone structures. For example, such an important building as the Taihedian (Hall of Supreme Harmony) in the Forbidden City had had to be rebuilt time and again after being destroyed by fire. Besides, wood grows very slowly and cannot be cut on a large scale recklessly.

2. Collective Layout of Structures

Traditional Chinese buildings are always found in pairs or groups, whether they are residences, temples or palaces.

The *siheyuan* (courtyard house or quadrangle) in Beijing is the typical form of residence in north China. It is a compound with houses around a square courtyard. The main house in the courtyard is occupied by the head of the family, and the junior members live in the wings on each side. This layout not only conforms to the feudal Chinese family moral principle of distinction between the older and younger, and male and female members, but also provides a quiet and private environment for family life. In the north, the land is vast and the population is not so large, and so the courtyards there are large, and the buildings one-storied; in the south—in Zhejiang, Anhui and Jiangxi provinces—there is comparatively little land for the large population, and so the court-yards are small, and the buildings two-storied and located on all four sides of the courtyards. This is called a *tianjing* (skylight) courtyard house. In the case of very large families, several *tianjing* courtyard houses can be connected to make a large residence with several courtyards.

Temples and palaces also sometimes display this layout. In the Forbidden City in Beijing, there are nearly 1,000 halls of varied sizes which are all grouped around large or small courtyards. Of these courtyards, the biggest is in the Outer Palace, formed by the Taihemen (Gate of Supreme Harmony), the Hall of Supreme Harmony, the Tirenge (Hall of Manifested Benevolence) and the Hongyige (Hall of Enhanced Righteousness). It has an area of over 30,000 sq m. In the Inner Palace

in the rear section of the Forbidden City, the Six Eastern Palaces and the Six Western Palaces were the residences of the imperial concubines, the empress and the empress dowager. They are all small-scale separate courtyards connected by lanes, and compose the largest palatial complex in the world.

In some mountain areas and other places with complicated landforms, structures or courtyards cannot be connected with each other regularly and symmetrically. They can only be laid out according to the local topography. In the mountain areas in southeast Guizhou Province, the Miao and Dong peoples build their houses on wooden or bamboo stilts. Built according to the rise and fall of the landform and arranged in rows with the mountain contours, these houses compose one village after another in picturesque disorder.

In garden architecture, in order to create an environment with hills and waters of natural beauty in a limited space, structures are usually carefully separated and laid irregularly to make variable spaces and different landscapes. Although occasionally grouped around courtyards, the pavilions, terraces, towers and halls are often separate scenes with a tenuous connection between them.

In both regular and irregular architectural complexes, decorative archways, pillars, screen walls, and stone lions and tablets besides small buildings play an important role in dividing space and forming scenes.

Most structures in traditional Chinese architecture are simple rectangles, and it is the architectural complex composed by single structures rather than the single structures themselves that expresses the broadness and magnanimousness of ancient Chinese architecture.

3. The Artistic Treatment of the Architectural Image

Ancient Chinese artisans ingeniously made the heavy roofs of buildings look light and graceful by forming the ridges and eaves into curves, and making the four corners stick up. The style of a roof can be divided into four basic types: *fudian* (wings), *xieshan* (hip and gable), *xuanshan* (suspended gable) and *yingshan* (hard gable), which denote a roof with a single layer, several layers, four corners and many corners. All these make the huge roof an important component of ancient Chinese architecture with an outstanding artistic image.

In order to impart lightness and grace to pillars, the diameters of the upper ends or both ends of upright pillars are slightly reduced, making them look like weaving shuttles. Beneath the pillars, stone foundations are needed to prevent humidity from underground eroding the wooden pillars. The foundations are often carved with decorative patterns. With the same purpose in mind, the two ends of the beams and crossbeams are given downward-pointing curves, giving them the shape of a crescent moon; thus they are called "crescent roof beams." The protruding parts of the roof beams are carved into various patterns, such as branches and leaves, and geometric figures.

The entrance doors of ancient structures are mostly made of wood with several upright wood boards connected side by side by horizontal wooden planks attached to them by iron nails. The heads of the iron nails are arranged on the doors in a regular order, and the color of the nail heads is different from that of the doors, which make them a special decoration. In addition, the knockers and handle rings on the doors are themselves made into ornaments bearing different patterns. It was only with the advent of the Qing Dynasty (1644-1911) that glass was installed in windows, replacing white paper. To make the pasting of the

paper easier, wooden window lattices forming various complicated patterns, including geometric figures and plants, were installed.

As for open-air terraces and their balustrades, whether made of stones or bricks, their foundations, the partitions between each balustrade, the column heads of the balustrades and other components are all carved with artistic decorations. Even the bricks and stones left over after the construction of houses are pieced together into different designs according to their shapes and colors, to decorate the grounds around the houses.

The decorations on ancient Chinese structures have cultural connotations as well as esthetic ones. The dragon heads on the edges of roof ridges signify the spurting of water to douse fires. The dragon, phoenix, tiger and tortoise were regarded as sacred animals by the ancient Chinese, and they carved images of them on eave tiles which were exclusively used on imperial structures. The emperors were supposed to be descendants of dragons, so there are images of dragons all over imperial structures, from balustrade column heads, terrace steps and stone foundations of pillars to roof beams, paintings on ceilings and carvings on doors and windows. Symbols denoting happiness, honor and longevity can be seen everywhere on traditional Chinese structures, including palaces, temples, gardens, residences, gateways, windows and roof beams. Bats represent happiness, deer stand for honor, and pines, cranes and peaches represent longevity. In addition, there are various patterns made by putting Chinese characters together, like the combination of the characters meaning happiness, longevity and ten thousand.

Ancient artisans were also good at using colors to decorate buildings. In the Forbidden City, stretches of yellow glazed tiles glitter under the blue sky, and there is a pleasing contrast between the dark green used beneath eaves, red doors, windows and walls, and white terrace foundations. Structures in private gardens in the south tend to have white walls, gray bricks and black tiles. Roof beams and pillars are usually left unpainted. Standing in harmony with the surrounding green vegetation, these structures create the simple and refined atmosphere beloved by the literati of old.

Wooden framework, collective layout and the artistic treatment of architectural image are the basic features of ancient Chinese architecture. In the following sections, we will get to know and appreciate the precious treasures of ancient Chinese architecture by introducing palaces, ancestral halls, religious buildings, gardens and local structures.

Palace Architecture

In the long history of Chinese feudal society, the emperors, as the wielders of supreme power, had palaces and other structures built which exalted them far above the rest of the populace. Thus, palace architecture represents the quintessence of the architectural techniques and esthetic aspirations of that epoch. Ancient records describe the now-vanished Epang Palace of the Qin Dynasty, Weiyang Palace of the Han Dynasty and Daming Palace of the Tang Dynasty as being huge constructions with broad courtyards, and magnificent halls, pavilions, terraces and towers. The only imperial palaces extant nowadays are the Forbidden City in Beijing and the Imperial Palace in Shenyang, which were built during the Ming and Qing dynasties, respectively. The Forbidden City in Beijing was completed in the 18th year of the reign of Yongle (1420). It was constructed totally in accordance with the traditional regulations of ancient Chinese palaces, and reflects the traditional features of Chinese palace architecture from the general layout to the specific appearance of structures and decorations. The Forbidden City concentrates the highest technical and artistic achievements of ancient palace architecture.

Tiananmen

Tiananmen (Gate of Heavenly Peace) was the front gate of the Imperial City in Beijing during the Ming and Qing dynasties. It was built in 1420, and named Chengtianmen (Supporting-Heaven Gate) initially. In 1651 it was rebuilt and renamed Tiananmen. This is a gate in the form of a rostrum with a grand tower situated on the wall high above with a double roof nine bays wide in the *xieshan* style of traditional Chinese palace architecture. A double roof denotes the building of the highest rank. In front of the gate, flowing from east to west, is the Golden Water River, spanned by five stone bridges, each of them facing one of the five gateways of Tiananmen. On either side of Tiananmen there stand a pair of stone lions and ornamental columns, which make the front gate of the Imperial City especially majestic and imposing.

Wumen

Wumen (Meridian Gate) is the main gate of the Forbidden City. It is also in the form of a rostrum, topped with a majestic hall with a double roof. On each side of the hall are two pavilions connected by galleries which jut forward. This layout shows the highest rank of a gate. Another Golden Water River flows between Wumen and Taihemen (Gate of Supreme Harmony), which gives access to the Outer Palace through stone bridges.

Hall of Supreme Harmony

The most important hall in the Forbidden City, the Hall of Supreme Harmony is situated in the center of the area reserved in the past for official functions. It is 11 bays wide—63.96 m—and 26.9 m

Inside the Hall of Supreme Harmony

Inside the central chamber of the Hall of Supreme Harmony, at the north end, there stands a throne with four gold-lacquered pillars twined by dragons. Beneath the throne is a wooden pedestal, and behind it are seven screens. There are dragon designs on the throne, pedestal, screens, ceilings and roof beams, symbolizing the divinity of the emperor as the "son of the dragon."

high, and built on a three-tiered stone terrace. Major ceremonies such as the enthronement of the emperor, celebration of the emperor's birthday and issuing of imperial edicts were held in the hall. At festivals, the emperor also received civil and military officials in this hall.

◀ The Coffered Ceiling in the Hall of Supreme Harmony

The coffered ceiling is situated in the center of the Hall of Supreme Harmony and look right above the throne. The lower edge of the coffered ceiling is square, and it narrows layer after layer, from square to octagon, to circle at the very top, from which hangs a dragon's head carved in wood and with a string of pearls hanging from its mouth.

The Imperial Ramp

The imperial ramp is part of the north entrance to the Hall of Preserving Harmony (Baohedian). Made out of a single block of stone, it is 16.57 m long and 3. 07 m wide, and weighs well over 200 tons. On its surface are carved nine dragons winding between sacred mountains, clouds and waters. The emperor, who was the only person allowed to use the ramp, was carried up and down it in a sedan-chair.

The Three Terraces in the Forbidden City

The three grand halls in the Outer Palace of the Forbidden City (Hall of Supreme Harmony, Hall of Central Harmony (Zhonghedian) and Hall of Preserving Harmony) all stand on three-tiered terraces, each of which is 8.17 m high. On every layer of each terrace there are balustrades, and beneath the balustrades there are dragon's heads carved in stone as water spouts.

◀ Qianqingmen

Qianqingmen (Gate of Celestial Purity) is the front gate of the Inner Palace of the Forbidden City. It is built in the shape of a palatial hall, with a hall five bays wide standing on a one-tiered stone terrace. In order to make the gate look more imposing, two screen walls stand on either side of it.

The Eastern Chamber of Yangxindian

Yangxindian (Hall of Mental Cultivation) was the place where the emperor slept and handled routine affairs from the time of Emperor Yongzheng. It was in the eastern chamber of Yangxindian that Empress Dowagers Ci Xi and Ci An held court from behind a screen, with the young Emperor Tongzhi sitting in front as a mere figurehead.

Imperial Garden

Located at the northern end of the central axis of the Forbidden City, the Imperial Garden was a place for the emperor to rest and amuse himself. In the garden there are pavilions, terraces and halls, amid a profusion of trees and flowers. In the picture is the Imperial Prospect Pavilion, which is built on a rockery, and was where the emperor viewed the moon at the Mid-Autumn Festival.

Ningshougong

Situated in the eastern part of the Forbidden City, Ningshougong (Palace of Tranquil Longevity) was prepared by Emperor Qianlong for his retirement. It is quite large, and divided into the outer and inner palaces. The front gate of Ningshougong is similar to that of Qianqingmen, and is also very imposing.

Corner Watchtowers

At each of the four corners of the wall surrounding the Forbidden City there is a watchtower in the shape of a cross in its plan view. The roof is a combination of layers in the *xieshan* style of traditional Chinese palace architecture, having 72 ridges in total.

The Imperial Palace in Shenyang

    The Imperial Palace in Shenyang, Liaoning Province, was the palace for Qing emperors before they went southward through Shanhai Pass. Dazhengdian (Hall of Grand Administration) and the five imperial pavilions on either side of it constitute the main structures. Dazhengdian was the hall where Qing rulers held ceremonies or discussed state affairs.

The Throne in Chongzhengdian

Chongzhengdian (Hall of Lofty Administration) was the place where Emperor Taizong held court and handled official business. In the center of the hall, a throne stands on a wooden platform. On the platform there is a special pavilion-shaped structure, whose roof, eaves and pillars are covered with carved designs, the two frontal pillars each being adorned with a coiled dragon.

The Coffered Ceiling of Dazhengdian in the Imperial Palace in Shenyang

Dazhengdian is an octagonal structure in its plan view. Inside, there are eight standing pillars with designs of golden dragons and clouds and waters, supporting an octagonal vaulted ceiling, bearing designs, the colors of which have now faded, showing the influence of Buddhism.

Altar and Temple Architecture

The worship of Heaven and Earth, the sun and moon, gods and spirits, and ancestors and celebrities was a principal part of the spiritual life of all ancient Chinese people, from emperors to commoners. Altars were set up to worship Heaven and Earth, temples were erected to offer sacrifices to deities, and halls and shrines were built to commemorate ancestors. The special styles of such edifices are indicated by the term "altar and temple architecture." Included in this category are altars at which emperors worshipped Heaven and Earth, the temples for the worship of Confucius, found all over China, and shrines to Guan Yu, a renowned general of the Three Kingdoms period (220-265), later deified. Temples and shrines for ancestral worship include the Imperial Ancestral Temple and a host of memorial halls for the worship of the ancestors of commoners, also found all over China. These altars, temples and shrines vary in shape from place to place and between ethnic groups.

Tiantan

Tiantan (Altar of Heaven or Temple of Heaven) was the place where the emperors of the Ming and Qing dynasties presided over ceremonies to worship Heaven. It is located in the southern part of Beijing. The main structures are Huanqiutan (Circular Mound), Huangqiongyu (Imperial Vault of Heaven) and Qiniandian (Hall of Prayer for Good Harvest). Looking northward from Huanqiutan, we can see that Huangqiongyu and Qiniandian are situated on the same north-south axis.

The Coffered Ceiling of Huangqiongyu

Inside Huangqiongyu, eight pillars support curved roof beams which constitute a triple round ceiling narrowing to a vault. Decorated with dragon patterns and the dark green of the coffered ceiling contrasting with the red color of the pillars, this ceiling is counted among the most beautiful vaulted ceilings in ancient Chinese architecture.

Huangqiongyu

Huangqiongyu was where the memorial tablet of the "Heavenly Emperor," the supreme deity, used to be enshrined. Situated on a round stone terrace, it is a round structure in its plan view, with a conical roof covered with blue glazed tiles. The round shape of the structure and the blue color of the roof have the connotation of Heaven.

The Coffered Ceiling of Qiniandian

Four pillars support the round vaulted ceiling of Qiniandian, which is painted in gorgeous colors. The pillars represent the four seasons.

◀ Qiniandian

Qiniandian was a place where the emperor prayed for good harvests. It is a round structure in its plan view, with a triple roof covered with blue glazed tiles. It stands on a circular three-tiered stone terrace. With the blue sky in the background, Qiniandian looks resplendent and imposing.

Confucius Temple, Qufu, Shandong Province

Confucius was ancient China's most famous philosopher and educator and founder of Confucianism. The main Confucian Temple in China is located in Qufu, the hometown of Confucius, in Shandong Province. Qufu is also where the former residence of Confucius and the tombs of the sage and his descendants are located. Emperors used to make a special journey to the Confucius Temple to worship the sage.

◀ **Taimiao, Beijing**

Lying to the east and in front of the Forbidden City, Taimiaio (Imperial Ancestral Temple) was the place where the emperors of the Ming and Qing dynasties worshipped their ancestors. The outer court of Taimiao boasts row upon row of cypress trees said to be 500 years old.

Decorations of the Ancestral Hall of the Chen Clan

The Ancestral Hall of the Chen Clan is famous for its gorgeous decorations as well as its large scale. The roof and wall ridges are decorated with pottery sculptures, and on the outer walls of the hall there are four huge brick sculptures with the themes based on ancient legends. Moreover, the stone pillars, stone roof beams and stone balustrades are covered with carved designs, and the doors and windows are decorated with wood and lime sculptures.

Ancestral Hall of the Chen Clan, Guangzhou ▶

The Ancestral Hall of the Chen Clan in Guangzhou is the central ancestral hall for all branches of the Chen clan in Guangdong Province. Besides its function as a place for worshipping the Chen ancestors, the hall houses a school—the Chen Clan Academy—for their descendants. The hall is in three parts, and has three large court-yards attached to it.

Zhuge Village Hall

Zhuge Village, near Lanxi City in Zhejiang Province, is inhabited mainly by descendants of Zhuge Liang, a celebrated statesman of the Three Kingdoms period. Located in the center of the village, the Grand Public Hall is specifically for the worship of Zhuge Liang. In front of the hall there is a pond and an entrance gate in the form of a decorated archway.

Village Ancestral Halls in Nanjing County

In Nanjing County, Fujian Province, there are ancestral halls almost in all villages. The ancestral hall is a place for families of the same clan not only to commemorate their ancestors, but also to hold public activities, get together on festive days, and conduct wedding and funeral ceremonies. In ancient times, ancestral halls played an important role in increasing the cohesiveness of clan members and managing public affairs, so they were larger and more beautifully constructed than ordinary residences.

▲ **Wenchangge, Xinye Village**

The people of Xinye Village, in Jiande County, Zhejiang Province, built Wenchangge (Pavilion of Cultural Prosperity) at the entrance of the village to pray for divine assistance for local people in the civil service examinations. The two-story pavilion with superbly made upturned eaves and corners dates from the 19th century.

Tomb Architecture

Generations of emperors paid special attention to the construction of their tombs and mausoleums, regarding them as palaces in which they would spend eternity. Hence, these imperial burial places were laid out somewhat on the lines of palaces above ground — the part for official business in the front, and the private part at the back, that is, halls for memorial ceremonies in the front and underground coffin chambers at the back. The counterparts of the civil and military officials who stood in rows in front of the emperor while he was holding court were men and animals carved in stone, including officials, horses, camels, elephants, etc., which form a magnificent sacred way leading to the tombs. The difference between mausoleums and palaces is that the locations of mausoleums are not in capital cities but in suburbs, where they are backed by mountains and face a vast prospect before them. The tombs of officials and well-to-do commoners display different formations and styles according to the historical era, and the various customs and traditions of different regions and peoples.

Terracotta Army Guarding the Mausoleum of Emperor Qinshihuang

The Mausoleum of Emperor Qinshihuang is located in Xianyang, Shaanxi Province. According to ancient records, this imperial tomb is deeply buried under the earth, and is a replica of the emperor's capital city, with palaces and offi-

cial posts, and countless treasures which have not been excavated yet. From the formations and large numbers of clay figures of warriors, chariots and horses in the outer part of the mausoleum, so far unearthed, we can judge that the tomb proper is of an unprecedented scale.

Qianling Mausoleum of the Tang Dynasty

In Qianling Mausoleum, situated in Qianxian County, Shaanxi Province, Emperor Gaozong and his Empress Wu Zetian of the Tang Dynasty are buried together. The site of the mausoleum is among the three peaks of Mt. Liangshan in Qianxian County. Leading up to the mausoleum, there is a 3,500-m-long path lined on both sides with stone figures of humans and animals.

All the imperial tombs of the Song Dynasty are located in Gongxian County, Henan Province. As the Song court ordered that each imperial tomb should be completed and the body interred within seven months after the emperor's death, the imperial tombs of the Song Dynasty are smaller than those of the other dynasties. Nowadays none of the original mounds of these tombs survive, leaving only stone figures of humans and animals lining both sides of the path to each burial place.

Ling'endian of Changling Mausoleum

Starting with Emperor Chengzu, 13 Ming Dynasty emperors were buried at the foot of Mount Tianshou, north of Beijing. Among the 13 imperial tombs, Changling, the tomb of Emperor Chengzu, is the largest. Ling'endian (Hall of Prominent Favor), the main structure of Changling, was where memorial sacrifices to Emperor Chengzu were held. It is also the largest hall in the whole of the Ming Tombs area. The pillars and roof beams of the hall are all made of precious *nanmu* wood.

The Grand Favor Hall of Dingdong Mausoleum ▶

One of the Eastern Tombs of the Qing Dynasty in Zunhua County, Hebei Province, Dingdong Mausoleum is the tomb of Empress Dowager Ci Xi. The Long'endian (Grand Favor Hall) in it was constructed using precious yellow-flower pear tree wood and *nanmu* wood. All the pillars and roof beams are decorated with designs of dragons, phoenixes and the Chinese character for longevity, done in gilt paint. The hall was constructed under the supervision of Empress Dowager Ci Xi herself.

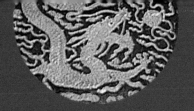

The Western Qing Tombs

The imperial tombs of the Qing Dynasty are located in two places—the Eastern Qing Tombs in Zunhua County and the Western Qing Tombs in Yixian County, both in Hebei Province. In these two locations, nine emperors were buried with their empresses and imperial concubines. At the entrance to the Western Qing Tombs, there are three marble archways. The archways are all five bays wide and made of stone, and bear exquisite ornamental carvings.

Changling Mausoleum (Qing Dynasty)

One of the Western Tombs of the Qing Dynasty, Changling has the same layout as those of the other imperial tombs of the Ming and Qing dynasties. In the front of the mausoleum is the entrance gate, in the center is the grand hall for offering sacrifices and at the back is the burial chamber. All these structures are placed along the same axis.

Changling Mausoleum (Qing Dynasty)

In Changling, besides the grand hall, there stand several small structures, including layers of outer walls, gates and stone altars, which increase the unity and coherence of the architectural complex, and create a solemn and respectful atmosphere for the mausoleum.

Zhaoling Mausoleum in Shenyang

This is the tomb of Huangtaiji, the founder of the Qing Dynasty. At that time, although the Manchu rulers of the Qing Dynasty had not yet crossed the Shanhai Pass and entered the Central Plain, their royal tombs had already adopted the traditional design of the Han-Chinese royal tombs, with a "sacred way" leading to the tomb, and entrance gate, grand hall and burial chamber, all standing on the same axis.

Tomb of Hasi Hajifu

Hasi Hajifu was a renowned Muslim scholar. His tomb is located in the city of Kashi. It looks like a mosque, with lofty pinnacled marble gates and minaret-style towers. The structure is entirely covered with blue and white ceramic tiles, lending a solemn air to the tomb.

Ancient Xinjiang Tombs

The Moslems of Xinjiang and other parts of the far northwest of China have long adopted a style of tomb that resembles the architecture and layout of a Muslim mosque. Characteristic of this style are round vaults and pinnacled marble gates.

Religious Architecture

The main religions of ancient China were Buddhism, Taoism and Islamism, of which Buddhism was the most widespread. As a result, Buddhist temples and towers are found all over China, and have become important components of the country's ancient architecture.

Buddhism came to China from India as early as in the Han Dynasty. Right from the start, Buddhist temples and pagodas adopted traditional Chinese architectural forms. For instance, the temples consisted of single-story structures built around one or more courtyards, often containing wooden or brick pagodas. Later, there appeared many other forms, such as the multiple-eaved design, diamond throne design and Lamaist dagoba design.

Taoism is the only religion which originated in China. The structure of Taoist temples and shrines is typically a traditional courtyard layout.

Islam came to China in the seventh century or so. Its temples are called mosques, which contain no pictures or statues. Disciples kneel and pray facing the holy city of Mecca. The mosques still keep the original pattern and style of those in the Middle East, making them special in Chinese religious architecture.

Thousand-Buddha-Cliff Grottoes

Grottoes are important features of Buddhist architecture. Work on the grottoes of the Thousand-Buddha Cliff near the city of Guangyuan, Sichuan Province, started in the fifth century. In its 873 caves there are over 7,000 Buddhist statues dating from the Northern Dynasties, Sui and Tang periods. Piled up, cave after cave, and facing a river, the grottoes look magnificent.

Guoqing Temple

Located at the foot of Mount Tiantai, in Tiantai County, Zhejiang Province, Guoqing (National Purity) Temple was established during the Sui Dynasty (581-618), although the existent structures were all constructed in the 18th century from the reign of Emperor Yongzheng of the Qing Dynasty onwards. It is said that the Tiantai sect of Buddhism originated in this temple. The eminent Japanese monk Zuicheng came here to study Buddhism in 804. He took back to Japan with him Buddhist scriptures, and established the Tiantai sect.

Grand Hall of Baoguo Temple

Located in the suburbs of the city of Ningbo in Zhejiang Province, Baoguo (National Protection) Temple is said to have been built in the Eastern Han Dynasty. But except for the main hall, built in 1013, all the present structures were built in the Qing Dynasty. The main hall is 11.9 m wide and 13.35 m long. The roof beams and vaulted ceiling inside the hall display the architectural style of the Song Dynasty.

Baoguo Temple

Mount Emei in Sichun Province is one of the four major mountains sacred to the Buddhist faith in China. Situated at the foot of Mount Emei, Baoguo (National Dedication) Temple is regarded as the entrance to the mountain. It was built in the mid-17th century, during the reign of Emperor Shunzhi of the Qing Dynasty, and is on a grand scale. The temple has three courtyards and several large halls. The whole temple is surrounded by mountains and woods, and is one of the representative Buddhist temples on the mountain.

Fayu Temple

Mount Putuo within the city of Zhoushan, Zhejiang Province, is also one of the four major mountains sacred to the Buddhist faith in China. It is actually an island, with three large Buddhist temples and dozens of small Buddhist nunneries. Fayu (Dharma Rain) Temple is large in scale, and has several courtyards and major halls.

Foguang Temple

Located on Mount Wutai, Shanxi Province, Foguang (Buddha's Light) Temple was one of the leading temples of the Tang Dynasty. Situated on a high terrace, the main hall of the temple is seven bays wide, and was built in 857. It is one of the oldest wooden-framed structures extant in China. The roof of the main hall slopes gently, with long eaves and big arches beneath the eaves, demonstrating the typical architectural style of the Tang Dynasty.

Hanging Temple

　　Located in Hunyuan County, Shanxi Province, Xuankong (Hanging) Temple is built on a cliff on Mount Hengshan. The temple was first built in the Northern Wei Dynasty (386-534), but the structures which remain nowadays were rebuilt in the Ming Dynasty. All the temple buildings, which are linked together, rest on horizontal timbers inserted into the cliff. This temple still stands firm, despite hundreds of years of wind, rain and earthquakes.

Puning Temple

Located in the city of Chengde, Hebei Province, Puning (Universal Peace) Temple is one of the famous Eight Outer Temples in Chengde. It was built in 1755, and displays characteristics of both Han and Tibetan styles of temple architecture. The main hall of the temple is the three-story Mahayana Hall, which contains a statue of a thousand-arm Avalokitesvara towering 22.8 m.

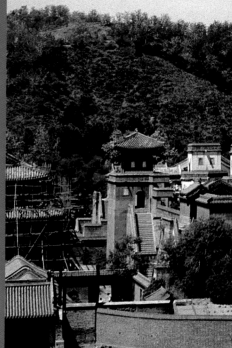

Putuo Zongsheng Temple

Located in Chengde, Putuo Zongsheng Temple is the largest of the Eight Outer Temples. Built in 1767, it is modeled on the Potala Palace in Lhasa. Its buildings match the topography. The main hall stands on a magnificent red terrace. Eight temples, including Putuo Zongsheng and Puning, and the Mountain Resort in Chengde are all on the UNESCO World Cultural Heritage list.

Id Kah Mosque

The Id Kah Mosque is situated in the city of Kashi in Xinjiang, being the most important mosque in that area. It was first built in 1442, and was rebuilt and extended in the Qing Dynasty. The prayer hall of the mosque is broad and lofty and can accommodate several hundred worshippers. In the corridor before the prayer hall there is an impressive entrance gate and vaulted ceiling.

The Octagonal Pavilion in Jingzhen

Located in Menghai County, Yunnan Province, the Octagonal Pavilion in Jingzhen is part of a local Buddhist temple. Its roof is actually eight groups of small roofs in the *xuanshan* style facing different directions. Hence its name. The pavilion is about 16 m high, with a delicate and gorgeously decorated structure characteristic of the architecture of the local Dai people.

The Wooden Pagoda at Fogong Temple

Wooden pagodas appeared soon after Buddhism took root in China, but the only early one preserved nowadays is the Wooden Pagoda in Fogong Temple in Yingxian County, Shanxi Province. Built in 1056, the five-story pagoda is 67.31 m high, and is the tallest wooden pagoda extant in China. In the center of the pagoda there is an 11-m-high seated statue of Sakyamuni.

Twin Pagodas in the Arhat Court

Wooden pagodas, being susceptible to damage from rain and fire, for the most part were soon replaced by pagodas made of brick or brick faced with wood. The Twin Pagodas in the Arhat Court in Suzhou, Jiangsu Province, are Buddhist pagodas of this kind. These seven-story pagodas are constructed of brick. Their roofs are made of wood, with their eaves upswept, which is typical of the architectural style of south China.

Glazed Pagoda in Zhaomiao Temple

Glazed pagodas are structures made of brick and covered with glaze to protect them from wind and rain. Such pagodas appeared all over China from the early Ming Dynasty. The Glazed Pagoda at Zhaomiao Temple on Fragrance Hill, in the suburbs of Beijing, is octagonal and seven stories high. It is entirely covered with yellow and green glazed tiles.

White Dagoba in Beihai Park

At the top of the hill in the center of Qionghua Island in Beihai Park in Beijing there stands a white dagoba, which was erected in 1651. It is typical of the dagobas of the Lamaist sect of Buddhism in that it has a bulging body.

Lesser Wild Goose Pagoda

A later type of Buddhist pagodas has progressively shorter stories above the second, bringing all the eaves closer to each other, giving such pagodas the epithet "dense-eaved." The Lesser Wild Goose Pagoda in the Jianfu Temple in the city of Xi'an, Shaanxi Province, is of this type. Built in 707, it had 15 stories originally, but only 13 remain. The pagoda is about 45 m high.

Qianxun Pagoda in Chongsheng Temple

Located in the city of Dali, Yunnan Province, Chongsheng Temple is situated at the foot of Mount Cangshan, facing Erhai Lake. Standing side by side in the temple grounds are three pagodas, which are regarded as a landmark of the city. Of the three, the central Qianxun Pagoda, built in the eighth century, is the main one. It is a square brick structure of dense-eave design, and has 16 stories, soaring 70 m. Visitors can get to its top by climbing the wooden stairs.

Twin Pagodas in Chongxing Temple

Chongxing Temple is in Beizhen County, Liaoning Province. Its Twin Pagodas are brick structures of the dense-eave design. The pagodas are octagonal in its plan view, their foundations bearing carvings of the Buddha and various decorative patterns. The two pagodas have identical structures, with the eastern one being 43.85 m high and the western one, 42.63 m. The Twin Pagodas are typical of northern China's Liao Dynasty pagoda architecture.

Manting Temple Pagodas

Manting Temple in Mengzhe, Jinghong County, Yunnan Province, is one of the principal temples in that area. The pagodas in the temple combine the styles of both Myanmese and Thai Buddhist architecture with those of the local area.

Qingjinghuacheng Dagobas

The stone Qingjinghuacheng Dabobas in Xihuang Temple in Beijing enshrine the garments of the Sixth Panchen Lama. The style of the structures, which were erected in 1782, is the diamond throne, which is one form of Buddhist pagodas. A large dagoba is situated in the center of a high terrace, with a small one at each of the four corners of the terrace. The dagobas are covered with stone carvings with Buddhist themes, reflecting the combination of the Buddhist cultures of the Han and Tibetan peoples.

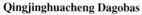

Manfeilong Pagodas

The Dai people of Xishuangbanna, Yunnan Province, are followers of Hinayana Buddhism, which was transmitted from Myanmar and Thailand. The architecture of the Buddhist temples and pagodas was influenced by the same sources. Built in 1204, the Manfeilong Pagodas in Jinghong County are typical local Buddhist pagodas.

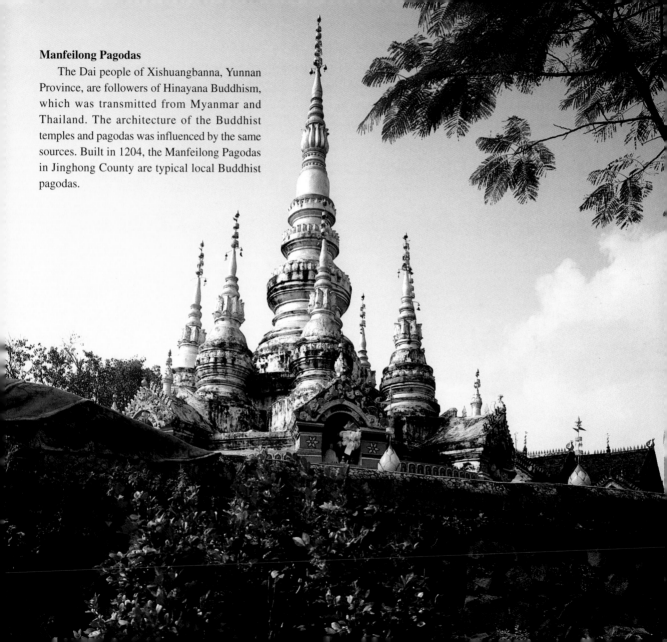

Garden Architecture

The most distinguishing feature of ancient Chinese gardens is their natural mountains-and-waters style. In a selected space, a miniature imitation of nature is created. In this environment, both body and mind can relax and be remolded.

All China's emperors liked to build their own imperial gardens. There, the emperor would handle state affairs, amuse himself and hold religious ceremonies. So imperial gardens are all on a large scale, containing palaces, and recreational and religious structures.

Covering smaller areas than imperial gardens, private gardens are mostly attached to residences. Within a limited area, the beauty of natural mountains and waters can be re-created by using the variation of space, imitating real mountains and waters, and constructing exquisite miniature structures. Throughout the ages, Chinese artisans built up a rich body of theory of garden construction, and bequeathed to posterity a lot of delicate and beautiful gardens.

Beihai Lake

Collectively called the Western Garden, Beihai, Zhongnanhai and Nanhai are broad expanses of water which were part of what was an imperial garden in the Ming and Qing dynasties in Beijing. Beihai Lake is located in the northern part of the Western Garden, with Qionghua (Jade Glory) Island as the center. On the island and the surrounding banks there are structures which form dozens of scenic spots of diverse sizes.

Jingxinzhai

Located in the northern part of Beihai Park, Jingxinzhai (Studio for Tranquilizing the Mind) is a small garden with a pond, rockeries, stone bridges, pavilions and terraces. The structures are artistically distributed, forming a wide variety of scenery.

Jianxinzhai ▶

Located in Jingyiyuan (Serene and Comfortable Garden) on Fragrance Hill, Jianxinzhai (Clear Mind Studio) is a garden inside a garden. In it, there is a pond with halls, pavilions and covered corridors around it. The garden is surrounded by outer walls, rising and falling with the landform, which make the garden both a separate space and a natural part of the surrounding hills and woods.

The Old Summer Palace

The Old Summer Palace (Yuanmingyuan) was the largest imperial garden in Beijing during the Qing Dynasty. Lakes and rivers occupy over half the area. The only remarkable relic left from those times is a unique marble boat.

Ruins of the Building of Exotic Delights of the Old Summer Palace

In the Old Summer Palace there were a group of European-style palace buildings known as the Western Buildings. In 1860, the Anglo-French allied forces burned the Old Summer Palace, and only some stones from the Building of Exotic Delights, which was a concert hall, remain.

The Summer Palace ▶

Built in 1750, burnt in 1860 by the Anglo-French allied forces and rebuilt in 1888, the Summer Palace (Yiheyuan) is one of the best-preserved imperial gardens in China. Its main scenic spots are Wanshoushan (Longevity Hill) and Kunming Lake. On Longevity Hill stand Paiyundian (Cloud-Dispelling Hall) and Foxiangge (Pavilion of Buddhist Incense). With halls, towers and pavilions surrounded by green woods, the Summer Palace still preserves the magnificence of the old imperial gardens.

Wufangge

Standing to the west of Paiyunge (Cloud-Dispelling Pavilion) in the Summer Palace, Wufangge (Five-Direction Pavilions) are a group of Buddhist structures. Looking westward from the top of Longevity Hill, we can see halls and pavilions close by, and green hills and woods in the distance. The Summer Palace has been put on the UNESCO World Cultural Heritage list.

Xiequyuan

Xiequyuan (Garden of Harmonious Delights) was built at the order of Emperor Qianlong of the Qing Dynasty in imitation of the Jichangyuan (Garden of Ease of Mind) in Wuxi, Jiangsu Province. Halls, pavilions and houses are scattered around a central lake, interspersed with rockeries built in imitation of scenes of hills and woods. It is a "garden within a garden" in the Summer Palace.

Lake Pavilions

In the lake area of the Mountain Resort there is an embankment with a lockgate for controlling the water volume between the east and west parts of the lake. On the embankment stand three pavilions.

Fangzhouting in the Mountain Resort in Chengde

Covering an area of 564 ha, the Mountain Resort in Chengde, Hebei Province, was built as a place for the Qing emperors to spend the hot months of summer. This imperial garden include palaces, lakes, plains and hills. Fangzhouting (Flowery Island Pavilion) is a square structure by a lake.

Xihu (West Lake)

The West Lake in Hangzhou, Zhejiang Province, is famous for its scenery, which is natural but has a touch of intentional landscaping. Small and neat gardens are scattered here and there.

The long and winding Narrow West Lake (Shouxihu) in Yangzhou, Jiangsu Province, is a famous scenic area in south China. The Windy Terrace is surrounded by water on three sides, and has a square pavilion. Through the round gate of the pavilion, bridges, pavilions and a Lamaist dagoba can be seen in the distance.

Fuzhuang on Narrow West Lake

On both sides of Narrow West Lake stand pavilions, terraces, towers and houses. Fuzhuang is a group of buildings which face the lake on two sides, surrounded by covered corridors and pavilions. Leaning on its balustrades, people can appreciate the scenery far and near.

◀ Geyuan Garden in Yangzhou

Built in 1818, Geyuan Garden is one of the most famous private gardens in the city of Yangzhou, Jiangsu Province. The garden is famous for its man-made hills. There is a rockery called Summer Hill. It is six m high and riddled with caves which afford cool shade in summer.

Heyuan Garden in Yangzhou

Heyuan Garden is a famous private garden in Yangzhou. It features towers and pavilions arranged around a pond, connected with each other by an unusual two-story corridor. Added attractions are exotic rocks and stone bridges.

Covered Corridor Beside the Water

To create a mountain-and-water environment in a limited area, the private gardens of south China often use covered corridors to divide the space. This covered corridor has water on one side and a painted wall on the other side. In the wall there are loophole windows, which divide neighboring parts of the garden from each other, yet they are not completely separated.

Zhuozhengyuan in Suzhou

Situated in the city of Suzhou, Jiangsu Province, Zhuozhengyuan (Humble Administrator's Garden) was built as a private garden in the 16th century. In the garden, there are 30-odd towers, halls and pavilions, scattered around ponds and on hills, and constituting different landscapes. Together with Liuyuan (Lingering Garden) and Wangshiyuan (Fisherman's Garden), Humble Administrator's Garden is one of the Suzhou Gardens, which are on the UNESCO World Cultural Heritage list.

Wufengxianguan in Lingering Garden

  Lingering Garden is a famous private garden in Suzhou, and Wufengxianguan (Villa of the Fairy of the Five Peaks) was where the master of the garden entertained guests. The structure is of unpainted wood. The furniture is also simple, yet exquisitely crafted, giving the villa an unsophisticated yet elegant atmosphere.

◀ Fisherman's Garden

Fisherman's Garden is a small private garden in Suzhou. In the garden there is a pond and pavilions, covered corridors, stone bridges and rockeries. The arrangements and colors of the structures were carefully designed, so the garden is tasteful and attractive despite its small area.

Zhuwaiyizhixuan (Bamboo Wand Pavilion) in Fisherman's Garden

This is a structural complex by the pond in Fisherman's Garden. The round Moon Gate, square loophole windows and a few green bamboos create a charming space in a narrow area.

Local Architecture

    Local architecture refers to structures built in the countryside, including temples, memorial halls, residences, stores, pavilions, bridges, decorated archways, wells, etc. Because these structures were all built by local artisans and villagers, and belong to the category of local structures, they are generally called local architecture. In local architecture, the country residences are the main type and the most numerous. Using local materials, the residences are built in the traditional local ways. Due to China's vast territory, numerous ethnic groups and regional differences, there is an abundance of different architectural styles. For instance, courtyard houses are called *siheyuan* in north China and "skylight courtyard houses" in south China. In mountain areas in Guizhou, Sichuan and Yunnan where there is an abundance of timber and a humid and hot climate, people build houses on stilts using local timber. In pastoral areas in Inner Mongolia and Xinjiang, where people travel from place to place grazing their livestock, their houses are in the form of tents called yurts which can easily be dismantled and put up again. In the loess highlands in Shaanxi, Shanxi and Henan, cave dwellings are built in line with local conditions.

Balustrades of *Siheyuan* Houses

    The village dwellings in Qinshui County, Shanxi Province, are two-story *siheyuan*. In front of the second story of the main house there is a carved wooden balustrade. In autumn, persimmons are hung to dry beneath the eaves of the house, a common sight in the locality.

The Grand Courtyard of the Wang Family ▶

The Grand Courtyard of the Wang Family in Lingshi County, Shanxi Province, was the residence of a wealthy merchant of the Qing Dynasty. It has several courtyards connected with each other.

Windows in Residences

The village dwellings in Jiexiu County, Shanxi Province, are also in the form of *siheyuan*. Between the pillars beneath the front eaves of the main house there are big windows letting sunlight into the rooms. By means of carved window lattices and paper-cuts, the local people create beautiful designs on windows.

◀ The Inner Courtyards of *Siheyuan*

The *siheyuan* of northern China usually have two courtyards each: the front one and the principal back one, which are separated by a gate (as seen in the picture) decorated with overhanging flowery patterns carved in wood. This arrangement makes the inner part of the residence a quiet and private space.

Hongcun Village

Hongcun Village is situated in Yixian County, Anhui Province. The main feature of the village is water: every house has access to a pond or stream. Hongcun Village and nearby Xidi Village are both on UNESCO's World Cultural Heritage list.

Huizhou Dwelling Houses

The Huizhou area of Anhui Province has been noted for its wealthy merchants since ancient times. As a result, tasteful residences have sprung up there. These buildings are in the form of skylight courtyard houses, mainly two-storied ones, with high walls. The white walls, gray bricks, black tiles, narrow alleys and entrance gates with brick carvings are features specific to dwelling houses in Huizhou.

Gate Decorations of Huizhou Residences

    The entrance gate of a residence is often the symbol of the owner's wealth and social status, and so it is common to see highly decorated ones. The entrance gates of residences in Huizhou are mostly decorated with brick carvings. Bricks are used in imitation of wooden beams, pillars and roofs and are covered with carvings reflecting wishes for happiness, longevity and honor. Decorations on entrance gates are called *mentou* (gate heads).

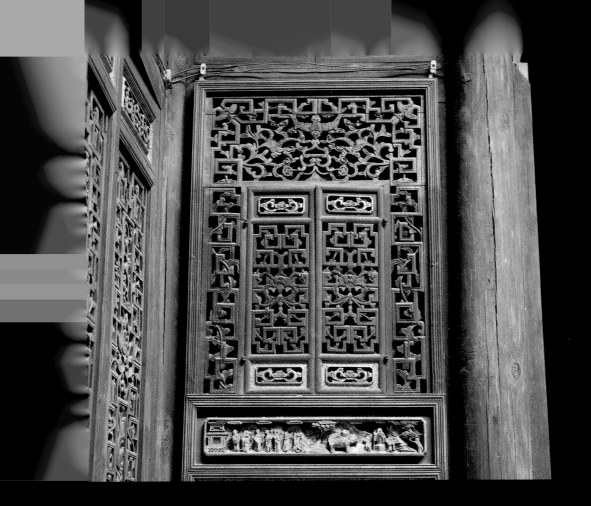

Windows of Guanlu Village

  Bedrooms of wealthy families in Guanlu Village, Yixian County, Anhui Province, often have windows covered with wood carvings. They only open slightly, so this kind of windows is more for decoration than for practical use.

Xinye Village

The inhabitants of Xinye Village, Jiande County, Zhejiang Province are nearly all related to each other, most people having the surname Ye. In the village, there are temples, ancestral halls, pagodas and a large number of ponds.

Typical Houses of the Miao People

The houses of the people of the Miao ethnic group, who live in compact communities in the mountainous southeast of Guizhou Province, are all built on wooden or bamboo stilts according to the rise and fall of the landform.

Yurts at the Foot of the Tianshan Mountains

On the plains at the foot of the Tianshan Mountains in Xinjiang, live scattered groups of nomadic Uygur and people of other ethnic groups. Their houses are in the form of tents called yurts, which consist of a wooden frame structure covered with felt. When the group moves on, the yurts are dismantled, folded up and carried on horseback, to be erected anew. The dark-colored yurts contrast strikingly with the green grassland around them.

Architecture of Other Kinds

Besides the above-mentioned palaces, altars and temples, tombs, religious structures, gardens and local residences, ancient Chinese architecture also includes the world-famous Great Wall, city towers and walls, shops, guild halls, theaters and stages, and decorated archways. These structures are found all over China.

The Great Wall

Work on the Great Wall, built as a defensive rampart against invaders, began in the third century B.C. Its basis was the existing walls built to protect the small states during the Warring States Period. These were linked up at the order of Qinshihuang, China's first unifier. The wall was continuously strengthened during the dynasties that followed. In the 17th century, during the Ming Dynasty, it was finally completed. It stretches from the Yalu River in northeast China to Jiayu Pass in Gansu Province in the west. It is 14,000 *li* (about 7,000 km) long, hence the name "Ten-Thousand-*Li* Great Wall." It is on UNESCO's World Cultural Heritage list.

Business Street in the Summer Palace

When the Summer Palace was built in 1750, a business street modeled on the typical commercial streets in the cities of south China was constructed inside it, along the river behind Longev- ity Hill. In 1860, this street was razed by the Anglo-French allied forces. In 1990, the shops along the river were rebuilt in their original style.

Pingyao County Town, Shanxi Province

The county town of Pingyao is over 600 years old. Its city walls with their towers retain their old appearance, and the old streets and stores dating from the Qing Dynasty are still preserved. Pingyao is on UNESCO's World Cultural Heritage list.

The Seven Decorated Archways of Tangyue

In Tangyue Village, Shexian County, Anhui Province, there are seven decorated archways standing along the main road. In ancient times, the decorated archway was a symbol of supreme honor bestowed on a meritorious member or a centenarian of a community. The most common decorated archways were those erected to honor widows who refused to remarry, which was considered to be a feminine virtue in feudal society.

The Theater Stage of Huguang Guild Hall

Guild halls were set up all over China by traveling merchants from the same province or native area. A guild hall usually included meeting rooms, a theater, a dormitory, office premises, etc. The Huguang Guild Hall in Beijing was built in 1807. Leading opera artists, including Mei Lanfang, performed here.

Sketch Map of Ancient Chinese Architecture

1 Tiananmen
2 The Imperial Palace in Shenyang
3 Tiantan
4 Wenchangge, Xinye Village
5 Changling Mausoleum
6 Tomb of Hasi Hajifu
7 Thousand-Buddha-Cliff Grottoes
8 Hanging Temple
9 Qianxun Pagoda in Chongsheng Temple
10 Manfeilong Pagodas
11 Fisherman's Garden
12 Hongcun Village
13 Fujian's Fortress Dwellings
14 The Seven Decorated Archways of Tangyue

图书在版编目（CIP）数据

中国古代建筑 / 楼庆西 著. －北京：外文出版社，2002.9
（中华风物）

ISBN 7-119-03115-5

I. 中... II. 楼... III. 古建筑－建筑艺术－中国－图集
IV. TU-881.2

中国版本图书馆 CIP 数据核字（2002）第 053048 号

"中华风物"编辑委员会

顾　　问：蔡名照　赵常谦　黄友义　刘质彬
主　　编：肖晓明
编　　委：肖晓明　李振国　田　辉　呼宝珉
　　　　　房永明　胡开敏　崔黎丽　兰佩瑾

责任编辑：蔡莉莉
英文翻译：陈　平
英文审定：梁良兴
摄　　影：楼庆西　翟东风
撰　　文：楼庆西
前　　言：楼庆西
内文设计：蔡　荣
封面设计：蔡　荣

（图片"秦始皇陵兵马俑"由中国文物交流中心提供）

中国古代建筑

楼庆西 著

ⓒ 外文出版社
外文出版社出版
（中国北京百万庄大街 24 号）
邮政编码：100037
外文出版社网页：http://www.flp.com.cn
外文出版社电子邮件地址：info@flp.com.cn
sales@flp.com.cn
外文出版社照排中心制作
北京大容彩色印刷有限公司·印刷
中国国际图书贸易总公司发行
（中国北京车公庄西路 35 号）
北京邮政信箱第 399 号　邮政编码 100044
2002 年（24 开）第 1 版
2005 年第 1 版第 2 次印刷
（英文）
ISBN 7-119-03115-5
05800（平）
85-E-546P